This book is a MUST R.
"Maintaining a Healthy Mar1
Daniel Abreo has produced a
& easy to follow techniques t.   , ...earched, & LIVED
in his own ongoing successful marriage!

Thurston E. Jennings IV
Company Mediator for Cakeboy & Cakegirl Inc. Charities

Daniel, I want to thank you for allowing me to review your book. "Honey if you leave me, I am going with you". The positive take on life that flows from your story is one that we all need to embrace. The improbable story of your romance would be hard to believe if I didn't know the truth of it! Your passion comes through. Many young (and old) couples will benefit from this advice. I know that it works. I have met the living products of your version of the romance/marriage process and all three of them embody all that I would hope for in a young man or woman. Thank you for sharing this document with me.

Maceo E. Cofield
UD School of Engineering

Daniel I have finished reading your book. Congratulations on your work. I enjoyed it very much. It is inspirational and aspirational. It is positive, warm-hearted and optimistic. You have reason to be proud of your effort and I hope that many people read your story. It will only help improve the reader's attitude and altitude.

Paul Oyaski
Attorney at law
Former Mayor of Euclid, Ohio

"In Honey if you leave me, I am going with you", Daniel Abreo openly reveals his passion for his beautiful wife and his unwavering belief in God. He shares with heartfelt insight the wisdom gained through the trials and tribulations of the marriage relationship, as well as raising a family. By taking Daniels's philosophies to heart, the reader learns the keys to sustaining a healthy, happy, and vibrant marriage in all phases of life".

Lisa Ryan
Author of "The Upside of Down Times" and "With Excellence"
"Chief Appreciation Strategist at Grategy®"

"This is truly an honest outpouring of Daniels's faith. While Daniel's theme is the sanctity of marriage, he touches on many areas of life so readers should not be limited to newly married couples or those experiencing troubles. This is Daniels's own love story—depicting his love for his God and the woman he wanted him to spend eternity with. Daniel shares his most personal thoughts and experiences—hoping they can be a living roadmap to a more complete and meaningful life for his readers."

All the best, and may God bless you and your family.

Peace, my friend.

Ray Somich
President, Spirit Media
Cleveland/Akron, Ohio Area, Marketing and Advertising

In a time where the institution of Marriage is quickly falling apart Daniel Abreo gives us hope in the beauty of lifelong relationships. The credibility of his insights, sprinkled with delicate humor, are evidenced in his own Marriage to his lovely wife Grace. We learn that what we share as married couples far outweighs the struggles.

Lisa Radey
Pastoral Associate
St. John of the Cross, Euclid, Ohio
Diocese of Cleveland

Honey, If You Leave Me, I Am Going with You

10 Points to Create and Maintain a Healthy Marriage

DANIEL O. ABREO

WestBow Press
A DIVISION OF THOMAS NELSON

Copyright © 2012 by Daniel O. Abreo.

All rights reserved. No part of this book may be used or reproduced by any means, graphic, electronic, or mechanical, including photocopying, recording, taping or by any information storage retrieval system without the written permission of the publisher except in the case of brief quotations embodied in critical articles and reviews.

WestBow Press books may be ordered through booksellers or by contacting:

WestBow Press
A Division of Thomas Nelson
1663 Liberty Drive
Bloomington, IN 47403
www.westbowpress.com
1-(866) 928-1240

Because of the dynamic nature of the Internet, any web addresses or links contained in this book may have changed since publication and may no longer be valid. The views expressed in this work are solely those of the author and do not necessarily reflect the views of the publisher, and the publisher hereby disclaims any responsibility for them.

Any people depicted in stock imagery provided by Thinkstock are models, and such images are being used for illustrative purposes only.

Certain stock imagery © Thinkstock.

ISBN: 978-1-4497-6520-0 (hc)
ISBN: 978-1-4497-6519-4 (sc)
ISBN: 978-1-4497-6518-7 (e)

Library of Congress Control Number: 2012915755

Printed in the United States of America

WestBow Press rev. date: 10/17/2012

Contents

Preface xi
Chapter 1: My Story 1
Chapter 2: God 12
Chapter 3: The Reason People Get Married 16
Chapter 4: Who Is in Charge? 23
Chapter 5: Our Differences 29
    Expressing Love 31
    Always Do Things Together 36
Chapter 6: Priorities within the Marriage 40
Chapter 7: Focus on the Good 46
Chapter 8: Intimacy 54
Chapter 9: Always Keep Improving You 59
    The Physical Part of Life 60
    The Mental Part of Life 67
    The Spiritual Part of Life 73
Chapter 10: Keep Improving Your Marriage 83
Suggested Readings 87

Dedicated to a beautiful lady who taught me the true meaning of love, my wife Grace. And to our children Jacqueline, Daniela and Marcos, they are our gift from God. To my Father the most humble person I have ever met, to my Mother, for her infinite wisdom. To my sisters Lilian and Adriana, two beautiful persons that I love so much. To my brothers in-law, Tono, Hugo and Angelo, and my friend Ariel Reynolds.

I want to publicly thank our friend Joe Narkin for doing the first editing of this book, for your time and dedication, I will always be grateful, to James Meyer from MRDigital, for the front cover picture of the book, and Mrs. Gina Tarantino for the final review. To Gennaro and Gladys DiNunzio for opening the doors of their house for me to stay.

Preface

Over thirty years ago, I came to the United States from Uruguay for two reasons: I was following my girlfriend, who came to the United States, and I wanted to see if this was truly the land of opportunity I heard it to be while growing up. I am happy to share my story with you through this book. Life in the United States has exceeded my dreams and expectations. This is the only country I know of that has had to build fences to keep multitudes of people from entering. Some people feel so strongly that life would be better in this country that they come in the trunks of cars, in the cargo area of trucks, in handmade boats, or through tunnels beneath the earth. I have even heard of one person who tried to enter the country via riding in the landing gear of an airplane. People from all over the world will do almost anything and take any risks for the opportunity to live in this country.

Many years ago, when the country was trying new things in order to improve the immigration system in the face of criticism over the way visas were being handled, the United States experimented with a visa lottery that was open to anyone in the rest of the world. All a person had to do was fill out an application and send it in. By the time the application period had ended, six million applications had been submitted. And I can guarantee you only a small percentage of the world's population even knew about the lottery in the first place. When the time came to pull out the winning applicants from huge barrels placed on a stage, television cameras transmitted the lottery to anxious applicants throughout the world who were praying and depending on their luck.

But what about you readers who are already living legally in the United States? You have already won the lottery! It is important for you to recognize how great this country is and all the opportunities it has to offer. The sooner you recognize how lucky you are, the better you will feel about your present and your future. Having a sense of gratitude is the first step in making things better in your life.

About two years ago, I had the good fortune to give a speech in which I shared my thoughts about how to live an inspired life. As usual, I was very excited about the message I had to share and grateful for the positive feedback I had received from the audience following my presentation. My excitement about giving a speech that was well received was accompanied by a feeling of humility over the fact that I had been given the honor of being able to share things that I know deep in my heart can help people have a happy life. I never take credit for what happens when I give a talk because, as I always share with my audience, I believe I am just a grateful messenger for the message God has placed in my heart.

As I returned home after that particular speech, I thanked God for the opportunity to hear his message and to share his wisdom. I also asked him what I could do to take my talks to the next level and reach more people. It was then that I heard a voice that told me, "Write a book."

While I am in the practice of listening to God's inner voice, I was still shocked at what I thought I heard. In total surprise, I asked, "What?"

The voice again said, "Write a book."

Part of my surprise at hearing this message is that I never went to college (except when I drove my kids to their schools), and my English is far from perfect, since my native language is Spanish. Naturally I was hesitant, and it took me two years to write this book. Sometimes we may wonder why everything takes so long in our lives, but most of the time it is because we do not listen to the inner voice that tells us what to do and when to do it.

The Scriptures are full of examples of people who hesitated to act in response to a clearly given message. The Israelites were captives in Egypt for four hundred years. During this time, they complained to God every day about how tired they were, asked him to show them a better way of life, and promised to do whatever he asked them to do if they could just get their freedom. So when God finally acted on their petition and sent Moses to lead the Israelites out of Egypt, what did they do? They grew tired of the harsh conditions and discomfort they encountered on the journey and started to complain to God after only two weeks. God became upset, of course, because the Israelites were complaining even though he was directing them toward everything they wanted. So instead of a six-week journey, God kept the Israelites walking around in circles for forty years before they reached the Promised Land.

I believe this is what we, God's creatures, do all the time. We ask God for something, and He begins working for us. But as soon as we encounter any difficulty, we complain to God. We quickly start to complain the journey is too hard, and God responds by making us walk in circles until we truly put our faith in him and let him take us there. I waited two years to obey God by writing this book, making all kinds of excuses. But despite making excuses that seemed legitimate to me at the time, I came to realize what we all must come to know: you can't fool God.

Perhaps one reason I procrastinated in writing this book was a crisis in confidence. Had I done enough of the work in my own life to justify God's confidence in me to write this book? It took me a while to understand the trajectory of my life and the fieldwork I had done under God's direction had led me to the point where I was ready to write.

I have been a devoted student of life and its spiritual dimensions for over twenty years. The thoughts and ideas I am about to share come from reading hundreds of books, attending seminars all over the country, and spending countless hours listening to inspirational tapes and CDs. I can probably count on my hands the number of days I did not do one of these things over the past twenty-six years in the interest of self-improvement. I believe the best investment anybody can make is to invest in oneself by spending time and energy continually trying to improve one's brainpower and also the ability to listen to the inner voice of God.

To this day, I have given over 750 speeches to audiences ranging from one person to thousands. Whether I am paid nothing or a lot, I always give my all, because I believe it is my calling, and it is a great source of happiness for me. My speeches usually consist of a message letting people know you can do better at life, and you must like yourself to take care of yourself in the way that God intends. In fact, other people are going to treat you in direct proportion to how you see yourself. What is important is not how your mother or father sees you, not how your brothers and sisters see you, or how your neighbors see you. What is important is how you see yourself. Do you like what you see in the mirror when you brush your teeth before you go to bed? Can you look yourself right in your eyes in the mirror and like what you see? The fact is most human beings, when reflecting on their lives, are not going to like what they see in their eyes through the mirror.

There are still people around me who do not know I am a public speaker. There are people in my life who make fun of my English, but it really doesn't bother me at all, because I can think back to times when I have gotten standing ovations following a speaking event. I can also think of times when people have approached me after a speech to tell me they appreciate what I do. And I can reflect on the times people have come to me, sometimes years after they heard me speak, and shared how I made a difference in their lives. I never take personal credit, however. I always try to point out to those who compliment me that God is using me to talk to them, and I feel blessed for that reason alone. All glory goes to God!

My own personal growth and desire to keep learning are what have led me to find my passion in life, which is to motivate and inspire others by sharing my story. I have been greatly influenced by Dale Carnegie's methods and my time with Toastmasters International. When I first started the Toastmasters program, I competed in speaking and became part of the Toastmasters International Speaker's Bureau. In 1996, Toastmasters asked me if I wanted to speak on behalf of the Mothers Against Drunk Driving (MADD) program, and I agreed. The director of the MADD program told me she loved my speech and asked me to speak again. I eventually became one of their regular speakers, sometimes presenting two or three times per week. As I write this book, I still speak on behalf of MADD.

I look back and realize I had some great nights, such as when I received a standing ovation. I wish there was a camera rolling on such nights. I feel honored whenever I have the opportunity to give a speech, and people tell me something I said helps them. Of course, there were more than a few nights when I thought, *That's it. Tonight is my last speech. Why am I doing this?* This usually happened when I was having difficulties in my own life, but on such occasions, at least one person would approach me to express appreciation for saying things he or she needed to hear. This is what has kept me going.

Despite some uncertainty regarding my English language skills, I am still amazed God gave me the inspiration and motivation to do public speaking and write this book. So many times, I thought God was playing a big practical joke on me in giving me this desire. But after many years of public speaking, I have finally come to the conclusion that God is not kidding. He really wants me to do this. I totally believe I was chosen by God to do what I do, which is to encourage people.

Throughout the Bible, God used people who, at first look, seem to be unqualified for the job of sharing his message. Even Moses, when he started, told God he could not do what God asked him to do. David was so small people didn't consider him as a future king of Israel. The apostles—the fishermen, the farmers, the tentmaker—seemed ill-equipped to undertake their assignments from God. I believe it is through such people that God best demonstrates his power. In other words, God knows how to make lemonade out of lemons. So I have decided to accept that God knows what we can and cannot do, and it is not my place to question his decisions. If God wants me, here I am. And for you, the reader, I hope you will be able to listen to God's voice and act on what he wants for you.

I also learned another important lesson in the process of writing this book. Like the Israelites came to learn, God's plans for us sometimes leads us in surprising directions, and the path to realizing God's plans for us can take some unexpected turns. I originally believed my job was to write an inspirational book about life in general. This is usually what I talk about when I give a speech. But during the last year of writing this book, I found I had an increasing desire to write about the things I believe are essential to maintaining a healthy marriage for life. And this is what I have tried to do.

This book isn't perfect, and I haven't covered all the thoughts I have about marriage. But as you read it, I hope you will find at least one or two ideas you can work on in your efforts to sustain your marriage during good times and bad. It breaks my heart every time a couple splits up, destroying their family and leaving children confused about life. My hope is if you are experiencing difficult times in your marriage (and don't we all), the thoughts and ideas presented here can help you find a way to stay together.

Statistics indicate that, in the current culture in the United States, 50 percent of the couples who get married wind up divorced.[1] I prefer to think of this figure in more positive terms and emphasize that 50 percent of couples stay married. A strong believer in the power of positive thinking, I believe you will get whatever you focus on. And the fact you are reading this book is clear evidence that you are interested in keeping your marriage vital and alive.

Life is like a roller coaster. Sometimes we are at the top and everything is great. But sometimes we are at the bottom, and things do not look too good. One of our goals when we feel we are at the bottom is to work toward getting back to the top as soon as possible. This is what I am trying to accomplish in this book—to give you specific ideas about how you can get your life and marriage back on track when you feel that you are at the bottom. Life never stops; our clock is always ticking, and we are either getting better or falling behind at any given moment.

---

[1] From "Marital Events of Americans: 2009" Issued August 2011. American Community Survey Report. By Diana B. Elliott and Tavia Simmons. U. S. Census Bureau

Although the reader may not like every point I make in this book, I have tried to do here what I do in my inspirational speeches. Furthermore, I hope to help you understand some of the basic laws that can help you live a spiritual life, which will then influence your marriage. It is often said that "It is not what you know that can hurt you, but what you do not know." Understood and used properly, these laws will work in your favor. If misunderstood or misused (and I believe that most people try to use these laws in the wrong way), these laws will actually work against you, whether you realize it or not.

I firmly believe the two most powerful ways to be happy is to be grateful for your blessings and to do things for others without expecting anything in return. I have tried to apply the principles of gratitude, service, and discipline in telling the truth in writing this book. I feel it necessary to point out that in all of the books, lectures, tapes, CDs, and DVDs I have used in improving my life, there is not a single guiding principle that cannot be found in a close reading of the Holy Scriptures, which includes principles that go back thousands of years.

The ultimate goal of any writer is to produce a win-win situation between the reader and the author. Writing this book has made me happy. If this book makes a difference in your life, I will be happy to know God has used me to help make that difference. I hope to offer inspiration through this book by sharing my personal story, giving advice on how to create and maintain a healthy marriage, and illustrating how to be physically, mentally, and spiritually in shape. Now I invite you, dear reader, to join me in an exploration of God-given principles designed to help you live a fruitful life and maintain a healthy marriage.

CHAPTER 1

My Story

I was born in Montevideo, Uruguay, on June 25, 1959, to Oscar Omar Abreo and Nelsa Raquel Toledo, my father and mother. I was the second of three siblings: Lilian, who is older, and my younger sister, Adriana. My father was a professional soccer player, who played thirteen years in the first division for Nacional and then Liverpool. He was also on the 1955 national team that played in the South American Championship in Chile. This was during a time when Uruguay had some of the best players in the world. That was a huge testament to how good he was. I have to confess I never really knew how good until I was a grown man. My father, one of the most humble persons I have ever known, would never comment about his successes in soccer unless somebody asked him. My mother was at home, taking care of the house and us children, which was so wonderful.

I grew up in the outskirts of the city, and we had a little, beautiful house next to the railroad tracks. I remember that the newspaper carrier used to ride the train and throw the newspaper from the train to land in our front yard. We had a dog, cat, chickens, pigeons, rabbits. We knew everybody in the neighborhood and were like a huge family with the neighbors. I went to public schools, because it would have cost too much money for me to go to a private one. I participated in any type of sport I could. But soccer was always my favorite.

In the fifth grade, I was on the school volleyball team. We competed against all the other schools in the city, making it to the finals. We were a very modest school; we didn't have even uniforms for the team. When we played the final, it was against a school that came from the rich part of the city. They came in a school bus, and they had cheerleaders, a band, and were all dressed the same. When we saw them, I thought we lost the game before we played. We were defeated in our minds by all the team's luxuries, which we were not accustomed to.

I was always a fast runner. When I started high school, there was a tryout to see who could qualify to compete in running so I did it and was the second-Fastest kid at my school. So they sent me to try out for what eventually would lead to the Olympics, but at that time the whole event was very disorganized. I had to go on my own to a stadium where they were holding the tryouts. I did not have a coach or anyone else from my school with me. When I got there, I felt so lost. I decided to leave and never go back again.

In high school, I studied enough to pass the courses and never did more than necessary. At the age of sixteen, I got my first full-time job in a factory and finished high school through night classes.

My wife and I have known each other since we were born. My mother and her mother lived across the street from one another and were girlfriends since they were teenagers. I was actually born into this world aided by a midwife in a house in the very same neighborhood. We still have a picture of my wife and I, standing next to each other at a birthday party when we were six and five years old.

When my wife, Grace, was nine years old, her family moved to the United States. Her father, a native of Italy, had moved to Uruguay, gotten married there, and had three children, before moving to join an uncle already living in Cleveland, Ohio. Four years after they moved, Grace's family returned to Uruguay for a visit. Like many families who have to travel far to go home for a visit, they decided to stay for an extended visit of six weeks. My family joined her relatives in greeting Grace's family at the airport. In traditional countries like Uruguay, it is common for friends to join family members at the airport to welcome or say farewell to those on a journey.

I vividly remember when their plane landed, and we were there to greet them. We were standing on a balcony at the airport and could see all the passengers going right under us and into the airport. Grace's father, mother, and brothers went by but not the person I was most anxious to see—the person who would soon turn my life upside down. Everybody else had left the balcony to greet the family, but for some reason, I remained behind to watch. I remember like it was yesterday how, when she suddenly appeared, I looked at her and thought, *Wahoooo!* It seemed like Grace and I were able to do no more than say "Hi" before we were back in the neighborhood. Grace and her family went to the homes of their relatives, leaving me behind.

A couple of days later, I went to visit my uncles and cousins, who lived on the same street where Grace's family was staying with relatives. It was a quick five-kilometer journey on my modified racing bike. I got in the practice of going there every day while Grace was in town. This led to organized bike rides with my cousin, Grace's older brother, and much to my joy, Grace herself.

I really liked her a lot, and I thought she kind of liked me too. One day, coming back from a bike ride, Grace and I stopped at the corner of her street, and gathering all my courage, I asked her if she would like to be my girlfriend. She said, "Okay."

Knowing she would soon be returning to the United States, I said to her with all of my heart, "I will wait for you for ten years."

Grace looked at me and said, "I will wait for you all my life."

Understand that, at that point, I was fourteen years old, and she was thirteen. At that age, ten years seemed like a very long time. On saying good-bye, I rode the five kilometers back to my house, not fully realizing I had just lived one of the most important days of my life, because that day, my life and Grace's had changed forever.

Two days after this momentous event, Grace and her family were going to visit her grandparents at their beautiful beach house. Realizing we would not see each other for a few days, Grace asked me for a picture of me that she could take with her. Not having a real picture, I gave her my ID, the only document I had in my possession.

When Grace and her family returned, I managed to show up wherever Grace and her family were. By then, her family, noticing that Grace was carrying my ID, knew we were up to something. Her family thought, however, that since Grace would soon be leaving, our childish emotions would soon be forgotten.

I clearly remember the day I showed up at the home of one of Grace's cousins for a dance party, a common type of event in Uruguay. Women show up with something they have baked, and the men show up with soda pop or some other kind of drink. While we were looking for chairs in a room separate from the main party, I found Grace next to me.

I gave her a kiss, my first mouth-to-mouth kiss and Grace's first kiss as well. It lasted about ten seconds. I have to tell you that a week earlier, I had broken three of my front teeth while playing soccer on a cement street. Needless to say, Grace's first kiss was memorable for more than one reason. She later told me I kind of hurt her with my broken tooth.

I liked going to visit when Grace was visiting one of her aunts, who happened to favor me. We would play cards with all her cousins. I would sit next to her and throw down all of the cards she needed to win. While this made Grace happy, it did not go over too well with her cousins.

When it came time for Grace to leave, I went with my family to the airport to say farewell. Part of me went with her. At that time, our respective families would say things like, "They are just two kids," and, "They will probably forget each other in a couple of months." I remember we kissed good-bye in front of all our relatives. It felt like they were all watching to see what was going to happen, but Grace and I were still able to communicate our love for one another in that kiss.

When Grace's family got onto the plane and took off, I was devastated. I went home and wept for several days, getting up only to eat or go to the bathroom. I listened tearfully to the songs we used to dance to while she was in Uruguay. My father told my mother he was afraid I was sick. My mother, however, knew what was really going on with me, and smiling, she told my father, "He will be okay."

Communication with the outside world was very scattered at my house, and links between Uruguay and other countries were also problematic. We did not have a phone in our home, so we communicated via the postal service, an agency that was slow and inefficient. I would write to Grace every two or three months, and it would take that long to get a letter back. Of course, there was no e-mail or Skype back then.

But Grace was always on my mind. I would frequently close my eyes and envision the moments we had spent together during her visit. I would often walk the streets of my neighborhood with one of my friends and talk about the time Grace and I spent together and how much I missed her. All in all, we didn't see each other again for five years.

After Grace finished high school and started working, I guess friends started to ask her out on dates. At that time, her father asked Grace if she was still interested in me. When Grace said yes, her father asked her if she would like me to come to the United States for a visit. Fortunately for me, she again said yes. So I received a letter, inviting me to visit her and her family in Cleveland. When I received the letter, I was incredibly excited and immediately accepted.

At that time, I had a very promising job doing payroll for a company with 120 employees. A man in the company became a close friend, a relationship that continues, and he had helped me move up in the company pretty quickly. I should also mention that the person who got me a job in the company in the first place was one of Grace's uncles, a very special, funny, intelligent, and fun guy to be around. When I received my visa and told my family, friends, and coworkers I was going to the United States, many people thought I had lost my mind. I was only nineteen years old.

Grace's younger brother, who was fifteen at the time, had come back to Uruguay to finish high school, but it was really hard for him. His Spanish wasn't 100 percent, and he was having trouble following the teachers. So he decided to go back to the United States, and we booked our flights together. Grace paid for my trip, since I couldn't afford the airfare.

It is customary in Uruguay to throw big going-away parties. Three parties were held in my honor: one with my coworkers, one with my friends, and one with my family. At the airport, of course, were the standard crowd of friends, coworkers, and family members to see me and Grace's brother off on our great adventure.

It was very hard for me to leave my country for the first time, but at the same time, I could not wait to see my sweetheart after such a long time apart. I remember that Grace's grandfather gave me a package for his son, Grace's father. I found out later it was a package of homemade sausages. I could not believe it, but back then it was a common practice among her Italian side of the family, but new to me.

Grace's brother and I arrived in Miami around 5:30 a.m., two young teenagers traveling together and having a great time. Prior to being allowed into the United States at the airport, we were interrogated separately by FBI agents, who wanted to make sure we weren't coming illegally or maybe bringing illegal substances into the country. We did not mind. After all, we were two teenagers coming to America by ourselves. There must have been red flags all over us, but it went well.

In the airport terminal, I asked Grace's brother how tall Grace was, because the last time I had seen her, she was the same height as me. He said she was not that tall. By now, I was 6' tall, but Grace was still 5'2", the same height as the last time I had seen her, according to him.

Our connection to Cleveland was not until 10:30 p.m., a seventeen-hour layover. Since we had the whole day, we decided to check in to the Miami Airport Hotel to shower, sleep a little, and get ready for the last leg of our trip. When we finally got to Cleveland at 1:30 a.m., there were not very many people at the airport. But it was at this time that another unforgettable moment in my life took place.

As we got off the plane and walked toward the exit, I saw this young girl running toward us. A security guard tried to stop her but without success. As she got closer, I realized it was my girl, my beautiful, beautiful girl. She ran into my arms, and we hugged and kissed. Emotions were running through me that I did not know I had. I realized there was never really a question about whether we were meant to be together. When Grace left Uruguay five years earlier, I believe we knew without a doubt that we belonged together—even if our families and friends had doubts because we were so young.

Eleven months later, Grace and I got married. Our wedding day was the happiest day of my life, and two weeks from the time I am writing this line, we will be married for thirty-one wonderful years. Thanks be to God! Grace and I have three children, and all of them have graduated from college and have promising lives ahead of them. We love them and are very proud of them. We are living our dream, a dream from a time Grace and I were just young teenagers, when we somehow knew we would get married, have kids, and live a good life together. Our early dream has become our reality.

But our dream did not become reality without a lot of work. Every good marriage takes hard work and commitment. Even though Grace and I love each other very much, we have had our share of honest discussions, disagreements, and hard times. But after all is said and done, as I write this book, I think I have not done too badly for a guy who came to the United States with a minimum of education and a need to learn a whole new language. But the reality is that throughout history, God always uses ordinary people for his great causes.

1965, Daniel and Grace (top middle) six and five years old, at cousin Alvaro's 2-year old birthday party.

CHAPTER 2

God

Surveys show that 90 percent of the people in the United States believe in God.[2] This also means that 10 percent don't know God exists. There are many religions in the world, but I believe most religions are talking about the same God. I wholeheartedly believe in God!

I believe in the Holy Scriptures. They tell me there is a God, and he created the earth, oceans, rivers, mountains, lakes, beaches, forests, and animals before he created man out of dust, reflecting his own image in man. According to Scripture, God created man to use his creation while exerting stewardship and dominion over all of the lands and creatures of earth.

---

[2] In the article, *More than 9 in 10 Americans Continue to Believe in God*, published on June 3, 2011, Frank Newport wrote, "More than 9 in 10 Americans still say 'yes' when ask the basic question 'Do you believe in God?'; this is down only slightly from the 1940s, when Gallup first asked this question."

It is hard to believe that out of an explosion everything in the universe was made, or that mankind once lived as monkeys but evolved into men over time. I would rather believe God created me as a creature with love and wisdom than believe I am a creature of accident. Even if I were to die and discover my beliefs were untrue, I would still be happy that the way I chose to live in accordance with my beliefs made me a better person.

My belief in God has helped me to achieve a healthy married life. I believe God is the glue that can keep a couple together, and without God in their lives, a couple's chances of staying together and being happy are slim to none. I see couples who are still together without a belief in God, but I find that they are miserable as far as marriage goes. Many people stay married even though they are not happy about it.

There are three main things that come from having God in your married life:

- God gives you love. Without him, you do not have love; so if you don't have love in your own life, how can you give it to anyone else?
- God also gives you wisdom. Wisdom gives you the ability to do the best with what you have and to make the right decisions in your marriage and your life.

- God gives us hope. Without hope, it is hard to live. God encourages us, protects us, and gives us peace of mind.

Whenever things seem to get out of control, I ask God to keep me at peace and to give me the wisdom to make the right choices. I also ask him for the discipline to do what I know I have to do. And I ask him for the sense of humor that allows me to enjoy the ride without taking life so seriously that I don't enjoy it. I believe everything happens for a reason, and if we trust God, we will believe everything that happens to us is ultimately intended by God to help us in the long run. The answer to the question of why is to trust.

Ultimately, the best advice I can give you is that you should do your best to do your part, and God will do the rest. If you go only halfway, God will go only halfway. It is up to you to do and be your best. Know that God always wants what is best for you, just like a good parent only wants what is best for his or her children.

I encourage you to take twenty minutes each day (morning or night) to pray and read the Scriptures. This is how we can communicate with God and strengthen our relationship with him.

1974, this is the day I ask Grace to be my girlfriend. She was thirteen and I was fourteen.

CHAPTER
3

The Reason People Get Married

This chapter is both for future couples to make sure they are getting married for the right reason, and for couples who are already married and going through difficulties. Perhaps you will see one reason that brought you and your spouse to this point, and you can work on the solution to help you move forward. There are many reasons people get married. However, there is only one reason for getting married that will keep you together when things get tough, when things aren't going the way you think they should be going, or when money is tight and your washing machine breaks. There is only one reason for getting married that will sustain you when the car's transmission goes out, when your insurance bill comes due, when your rent goes up, and when everything seems to be falling apart.

Some people get married because:

- They feel they are old enough to start a new life and believe getting married is the way to do it.
- They want to get out of their parents' home and believe getting married is what adults do.
- Their friends are getting married.
- They have found someone who seems to have it together financially and appears to be the best candidate to avoid financial problems in the future.
- They find a person who is beautiful and want others to envy them for having a beautiful spouse.
- They are not so sure the other person is best for them, but believe that, once they are married, they can change the other person into the kind of person they would like them to be.

From the time that they get engaged, some people focus on the day they will get married and start planning a wedding date, party arrangements, a guest list, a wedding budget and who will pay for it, and their honeymoon. Some people get so involved in planning for the wedding that they lose sight of what is really important, including the needs of the person with whom they expect to spend the rest of their lives. I believe this is one of the major reasons that, after one or two years of marriage, some people realize they did not marry the right person and are not going to be able to change their spouse to be what they wanted him or her to be.

At this point, many spouses begin to complain to friends that the other person is different than they thought he or she would be or that the other person changed after getting married. The real problem is such people may have been so blinded by the idea of getting married that they saw what they wanted to see, or they were blind to what they didn't want to see. Some spouses are crushed by the reality of living every day with the other person once the wedding is over. Their eyes are finally open, and they can see what they have gotten themselves into.

Faced with disillusionment, some people start looking outside of their married life for solutions to their problems. They talk to other people about their marital problems and ask others for solutions. When looking for answers, only talk to people who already have a great marriage. Some people believe having children and starting a family will be the solution to their difficulties.

It is only when a couple enjoys each other's company and has a great time together that having children will make things better. But one of the most important things every married couple should know is that having children will only amplify your situation. If a couple is having differences and things are not too good in the relationship, having children is going put more stress in the relationship. But don't forget that children are a gift from God, and God will not give you a gift you cannot handle.

Some people may get married because they are serving in the military or have some other type of long distance relationship. In such circumstances, a person may think getting married will lock in their relationship, and they will not have to worry about losing the other person.

In my opinion, the only reason to get married is if you are madly in love with one another. I say with each other, because the feeling must be mutual. When such love exists, nothing else matters, and everything will fall into place. When love exists, everything else will come second to the magnificent feeling that exists between married couples.

Grace and I became boyfriend and girlfriend in our early teen years, but we did not see each other again for over five years. Even though we both had countless opportunities to date other people, the seeds of love were already planted in our hearts, and we knew we were together no matter how many miles separated us, no matter what circumstances we were in.

Love! You cannot force it. You cannot create it. You cannot chase it. Love is an invisible force that will grab you at the right time and the right place. For my wife and I, it was at an airport during our early teens. But love will come differently for everybody. All I know is that when Grace left town to return to Cleveland, I could not sleep or think. My whole world was changed. When you are in love, you come alive, you are in a cloud, and you feel great about everything. You cannot stop thinking about the other person for even a single moment. After Grace left from her visit in Uruguay, my father thought I was sick, but my mother know I was fine. She knew I was in love.

For the single person who is wondering if he or she will ever get married, what I am trying to tell you is that you should not be out there searching for your prince or princess. If you just live your life and do the things you like to do, you will meet the right person when you least expect it. Everything in your heart will tell you when you have found love, but the truth is that love will have found you.

Some people go to bars to try to find the right person. Desperate to find the right person, some go to dating services and on blind and forced dates. I say you cannot force love to come to you, but you can allow it to come to you by making the best out of your life. If it is meant to be, love will find you. If you are getting old and love hasn't found you, do not be discouraged. See what habits you need to change, ask God for what you want, and allow it to happen.

What I suggest is in allowing love to come into your life, you consult the best matchmaker you can find. It is a matchmaker who knows your heart inside out and who knows what is in the hearts all other people. Get on your knees in respect and submission, and ask your Creator to send you the person who you will want to spend the rest of your life with. When you have done so, stop thinking about finding love, and know your petition was heard.

Imagine a farmer who plants the seed of a tree, a farmer who covers it with soil and waters it regularly. Imagine that after a week, the farmer does not see anything growing and uncovers the seed to see if anything is going on. Then he covers it again and waters it, but after a month is troubled that he does not see anything growing. He digs it up again to inspect the process. Do you think that is helping the situation?

What he is actually doing is disturbing the natural process that allows a seed to grow into a beautiful tree. He may be actually killing the seed, because he is not giving it the time necessary to develop as it must to transform itself. In such a case, the farmer is acting in anxiety and mistrust; his lack of faith guarantees he will never see the magnificent tree he desires.

The same dynamic applies to us in allowing love to come into our lives. Once we ask God for what we want, once we plant the seed, we must continue our lives, and at the right time, it will happen without effort on our part. Love will come to us naturally when we seek it through God, just as a tree will grow in the forest without any help. That is the way of love and of life.

1974, Grace was coming back to the United States; this is the airport in Montevideo, Uruguay. After this we didn't see each other for five years.

CHAPTER
4

Who Is in Charge?

According to the Scriptures, God created the first man, Adam, but realized he was lonely. So God put Adam to sleep and, out of his body, took one of Adam's ribs. From that rib, God created Eve, the first woman, to help Adam and be his companion. This is why, in biblical times, men gathered together to make important decisions. Men and women complemented each other, but the man of the house always had the last word. While men looked to God for guidance, women looked to men for their guidance.

This does not mean the "macho" man is in charge, however. To the contrary, a good husband will take care of his wife, while a good wife will fulfill all of her husband's needs. The two work together toward mutual goals.

Today, unfortunately, some men are too lazy to take on the responsibility of being in charge, forcing women to take over this responsibility. Consequently, a man who gives into such laziness is going to fail, and diminished in his human destiny as a male, he will be incapable of supporting a good married life. This does not mean a man has to be like a dictator, operating under his own sense of power. Rather, a man should get on his knees every day and ask God to help him make the right decisions for his family.

I also believe a woman who knows she is married to a man who is not afraid to take on responsibilities will feel secure. When a woman marries a man who is afraid to meet his responsibilities, she will not be able to respect him and will take control. There is a very fine line that such a woman will need to walk. On the surface, it will seem like she wants to be in charge, but in reality, she would prefer her spouse to take charge. A woman likes to know she is married to a man rather than a mouse. In this case, it is important to put all the cards on the table and talk about it. See if he wants to reconsider and do his part in the marriage. If this does not work, I highly recommend going to a professional counselor.

A woman has more power than she knows in married life, because when we men get married, it is like a little switch turns on inside us that makes us wish to fulfill our wife's desires and make her happy. So the wife has the ability to actually control the marriage by knowing what she wants and when she wants it. It goes like this. Say a husband and wife are having a casual conversation, and the woman says, "I would like to go on vacation to the beach." At that moment, the husband's inner switch turns on, and he starts to think about what he must do to take his wife to the beach. If the wife says she wants a particular type of car or a bigger house, the husband will automatically begin to strategize how to make the things she wants to happen.

Now this is the way it will happen under a marriage that is going well. But if things are not going well in the marriage, these could be perceived as demands, which men will not respond to. In fact, some of them will do the opposite to prove they have control. In the latter case, you need to sit down and talk over how you both feel about your marriage.

This is why it is very important for a wife to think about what she really wants before making her desires known. If a wife is actually steering the boat but is constantly changing directions, the boat will not travel too far. I believe many couples have trouble, because the wife changes her mind. Or the husband may misunderstand what she wants, and this makes the husband become confused about what she wants. Such a husband will find himself going in too many directions and may stop trying to please her. Here again, setting goals together for your marriage would be of great benefit.

I think one reason this happens is because a man is more attuned to long-term thinking, always planning five to ten years into the future, while a woman tends to think in terms of now and the next six months. Thus, it is very important for spouses to understand how each other tend to think and what they want out of their marriage. This way, they can deal with each other better.

It is also important for spouses to communicate and explain their thinking to each other. It's been always difficult for me to realize that each person is going to look at a situation from different angles. We are all different (thank God). We grow up differently and we learn differently, so when we look at the same situation, we may see different things. That's the reason more than one referee is used in many sports, and sometimes they stop the games to talk about what each other saw from the angle they were positioned at. In my house, I have the habit of always putting the toilet paper to come from the bottom, because I believe doing it that way will make it come a little slower than coming from the top, so we will waste less paper. That is not how my wife sees it. I believe you should start moving your car slowly before turning your front wheels, because I believe this is better for the car. She doesn't see the benefit of this. All too often, when a husband makes decisions, his wife will not understand why. And on the other hand, a husband may not understand his wife's decisions. The reason for such misunderstandings is that the husband and wife do not understand each other's timetable for the future.

Nobody said it was going to be easy, but nothing worth working for is too hard, either. The sooner you and your spouse make the decision you are married for life rather than just waiting to see what happens, the better married life will work for the two of you. I believe when a couple is totally in love with each other, they will constantly work together to fulfill their appropriate roles in a marriage. They will achieve a level of happiness in their marriage that few people have the opportunity to enjoy.

1977 with my father in the back of our house. We were playing soccer for the same team Boca Juniors in Uruguay, he played for the veterans and I for the juniors.

CHAPTER 5

Our Differences

In an ideal situation, a married couple is going to be like a picture puzzle. When the puzzle of marriage is put together, you see a picture of a perfect family, where everybody is working in harmony. If you take the puzzle apart, however, and look at each piece separately, it is hard to see how all the individual parts can come together to form a beautiful picture. One cannot see the whole picture by only looking at the parts. But it is important to realize when combined in the right way, the picture is there.

Men and women are so different in all areas, but those differences, when combined correctly, make a beautiful picture. It is often said that differences attract. Maybe this is because men and women feel incomplete and look to each other to become whole. When you find your mate, all the pieces of the puzzle will fall into place. Knowing this is fundamental in making a marriage work. And it does take a lot of work to make a marriage work. But it is worth it—every minute of it.

I believe a husband cannot outdo his wife in what she does for the family, because as I have said, she was created by God to help her mate. So whatever you do, she is going to do more for you than you can do for her. But make sure that whatever you do, do it out of love for her and a desire to make your relationship the best it can be. Try these things, and you will be amazed at what will happen to your marriage.

Men have a tendency to be rough and tough, while women are soft and sensitive. Husbands are okay if the wife does not tell him she loves him, but a wife needs to be told of her husband's love as often as possible. Husbands can see a wife's love in the actions they take, but a wife must see the actions as well as the words that accompany love. A wife needs to hear she is beautiful, her hair is awesome, her clothes look fabulous, and she is sexy. She needs to hear she is a great wife, a fabulous mom, and an incredible person as often as possible. A wife needs to be told she knows how to take care of her husband in all areas of his life. She needs to hear she is the perfect wife.

What a husband needs in a wife is something like a cheerleader—someone who believes in him, even when he makes mistakes. A husband needs a wife who thinks of him as a hero, who believes her husband can conquer the world, and that great things are just around the corner for them as a couple.

A woman likes to be treated like a lady and with gentleness. At every opportunity, a husband should open doors for her, whether it is the door of a car or the door of a restaurant. He should help her on with her coat, move her chair out for her, and carry heavy things for her. Such little things mean a lot to her, even if she does not say so. For a wife, every action you take, every word you say, and every encounter you have with her will bring her closer to or further apart from you. From the moment you get up in the morning, the way you talk to her and treat her will determine, in a big way, how the day between you and her is going to go.

Expressing Love

You should find out what your spouse likes, so you can work on accomplishing the things that are going to work in your marriage. This is not a complete list; I am just giving some ideas for starting to work toward your healthy marriage.

***Imagine if* . . .**

- The first thing you say to her in the morning is that you are very much in love with her, that she looks more beautiful every day, and that you are the happiest and luckiest man in the world for having her as your wife.

- When you come into your house and she happens to be cooking or doing dishes, you hug her from behind, kiss her on the neck, tell her she is awesome, and let her know you appreciate everything she does for you and the family.
- Every once in a while, you buy her a nice card, write of your love in it, and place it where she is certain to find it. How about asking her if she needs help with anything when she is doing chores around the house.
- How about you as a wife: smile when you see your husband, and tell him how happy he makes you.

One thing that is precious for me is when I see my wife smiling, and she tells me she loves and believes in me, she is happy I am hers, I am her man, and she looks forward to spending the future together.

Don't forget flowers, even if she says that she does not care about such things. How about a candlelight dinner at home? Or you can go out and make it her special night by taking her to her favorite restaurant and going to a movie she really wants to see. Believe me when I say your wife will greatly appreciate such things, and you will be happier.

Whenever your wife talks to you, make sure you stop what you are doing and listen. After all, isn't your wife the number one person in your life? When your boss talks to you at work, you stop and listen, don't you? Who is more important to you than your wife?

Patience is huge in a marriage. We tend to expect more of the people we love than from anyone else. This is why we tend to argue more with our family members. We may put up with all kinds of things from our coworkers. But when one of our family members does something or says something we do not like, look out world! We go insane.

Imagine if God had the same level of patience with us as we have with our family members, especially with our spouses, when they don't do something they were supposed to do or when they make a mistake. When a husband and wife want to spend the rest of their lives together but get frustrated by disagreements, they should give each other the space to think things out and come to a compromise.

What a husband needs to know is that a wife sees him as her man. He needs to know she believes in him and that he is number one in her life. A wife's parents may have been number one in her life up to the moment she got married, but when she chose her husband, she chose him to be number one. A wife's parents are always going to have an irreplaceable part in her life, and this is only natural, but she must remember she now lives with her husband. It is natural for parents to want the very best for their children, so when their kids get married, they naturally tend to try to help. Sometimes it's too much, whether his parents or hers. In either case, we need to break the umbilical cord and start our new life. Even if we make mistakes, we will learn together. And we need to sit down with the parents while doing this and let them know we appreciated what they have done and what they are trying to do, but they need to respect your lives, and let you do things in your own.

Speak well of each other. Never call each other a bad name or swear at each other. Harsh words that come out of your mouth can cut like a knife, cause a stabbing pain, and leave a scar that will not easily go away. Never complain or talk critically about your spouse with other people, whether they are family, friends, or coworkers.

What you talk about will become stronger through the law of attraction. Doesn't it make sense to talk about the good things in your marriage while knowing this will attract better things to your marriage. Talking about the things that are not so good can make the not so good things even stronger. And the person you are telling about your marital problems probably doesn't care anyway, because he or she is probably concerned only with what is happening to them.

I often see coworkers who talk about their spouses like they are a piece of dirt. In many cases, what they are really saying is they made a huge mistake when they married their spouse. In some cases, they are admitting they do not know how to make their marriage work. In either situation, they are putting themselves down and don't even know it. In other words, when you put down your spouse to others, the only person you really put down is yourself.

Never be afraid to tell others how much you enjoy your marriage. People need to hear such positive things about marriage. As I am writing this book, Grace and I have been married for thirty-one wonderful years. I always talk about my marriage in this positive way because I want people to know a marriage can work if you work at it.

A wife needs to tell her husband how strong he is, how sexy he looks, and how lucky she is to have him. He needs to know his wife wants to be intimate with him. A wife needs to encourage her husband to follow his dreams. I will let you in on a secret. A husband's dreams are always going to include what is best for his wife. For a husband to be happy, he needs to see that his wife is happy, or he thinks he is failing. In my own marriage, my greatest moment is when I see Grace with a smile on her face. Nothing can make me feel better.

You can tell your husband, "I am so glad I married a lion and not a mouse." This will help him go out and conquer the world. I often see couples who put each other down and then wonder why their marriage is going down the tubes. Whenever you walk together, you should hold hands and show that you are in love and happy to be together.

How about if, for no reason, you give your spouse a foot massage? Remember always the old saying, "If you don't tell your spouse that you love them, somebody else will"? If you don't make your spouse feel good, somebody else will. If you don't believe in your spouse, somebody else will believe in him or her. If you don't trust your spouse, somebody else will trust him or her.

Always Do Things Together

Always do things together because the reason you got married was to spend your lives together. I remember when Grace and I got together and she would go with me to soccer practices. She would often be the only wife in the stands, watching us play. For us, it seemed normal to be together in this way.

If you are currently living together, commit to each other and get married. If you are not sure about getting married, it means you should not be living together, because you are wasting your time. You either love each other or you don't. All you are doing is playing "hokey pokey." You put your right foot in or take your right foot out, depending on how you feel on a day-to-day basis. What a way to live, when you never know if you are going to be together next month.

Once you are married, you cut the umbilical cord with your parents and your friends. Now if you want to go out and have a good time, you should take your spouse with you. When you start going out with old friends who are single or who may be having problems in their own marriages, you will be tempted to do things that could compromise your own marriage. It is not worth it. There are special occasions when you or your spouse will go out on his or her own, like an all-female luncheon or a Boy Scout meeting, but make this the exception and not the norm.

When you are joined together in marriage under God, the only acceptable way, as far as I am concerned, is for you and your spouse to do everything together and to join your lives together fully. I don't understand when a married couple says, "I pay these bills, and my spouse pays other bills." What? Now that you are married, you join everything together. You should use the same bank, the same credit card, and the same money—unless one of the two is totally irresponsible with money or has a gambling problem and agrees for the other to take complete control of the money. Nothing should be hidden from each other. If you find yourself in a situation where each has a different bank account, try talking about it to see if it will be possible to merge them, and start sharing the money responsibilities so the two of you know what's available.

If you do not trust your spouse 100 percent, it is not going to work. Trust comes right after love as a critical element in a marriage. Grace and I share everything. We share our goals in life, and we help each other accomplish these goals. Some men or women go on vacations with their friends and leave their spouses at home. Why not bring them along? After all, the reason you got married was to be together. I believed if the reason your spouse is left behind is because it will be too expensive for you both to go, then you shouldn't go. And if your spouse doesn't like where you are going, find a place where both of you can have a good time. The saying "What happens in Vegas stays in Vegas" does not apply for Vegas alone. Now if you don't want your spouse to go along on vacations, it is your choice. But remember that temptations don't sleep. The more things we do together, the healthier the marriage.

    These are just some ideas of things you can do to make your marriage the best it can be. You don't have to do exactly what I suggest, but I hope I have been able to give you a general idea about how to work at creating and maintaining a healthy marriage. Maybe you are already doing a lot of the things I have suggested. If so, that is great. But I hope I have been able to offer one idea in this chapter that will make a huge difference in your marriage.

1978 with my sisters Lilian and Adriana in a park in Montevideo.

CHAPTER
6

Priorities within the Marriage

Once you are married, you are going to have to make many adjustments. Your goal should now be to become the best spouse possible, and the goal should be the same for your spouse. Reading books on the subject and going to seminars will help you define what your goals should be and how to achieve them. Talking to couples who have been married for a long time and are happily married is also a good source of guidance. If you and your spouse are working toward the same goal, your chances of having a great marriage are fantastic.

When couples get married and dedicate themselves to each other, they usually decide to start a family and complete their dream through children. This is what makes a family complete. Even though many married couples limit the number of children they have for economic reasons, studies have confirmed that married couples are more satisfied with their lives when they have more children.[3] But when a married couple starts having children, it is very important that the priorities of the marriage stay the same. This means the husband must be the number-one priority for the wife, and the wife must be the number-one priority for the husband. The husband and wife come before the children always. I believe God is always number one for both, but I am now talking within the married life. Once they start having children, many couples make their children the number-one priority, putting their spouse in second place. This does not work very well. Married parents need to keep fulfilling each other's needs, and the children will easily adjust when that takes place.

When a spouse makes children the number-one priority, the other spouse may feel neglected. This can often be the start of a failing marriage. After all, the spouse was there first, and after the children have grown and left the nest, the spouse will still be there. After you start having children, it is important to maintain a lifestyle similar to that which existed before bringing kids into your relationship. You should continue to do things as a couple, like going out to a movie once a month or more. Such periodic renewal will allow you to keep your relationship fresh and growing, while you are also working together to help your children grow. A couple

---

[3] "More Kids = More Happiness?" by Bonnie Rochman, posted November 6, 2009, on www.slate.com.

must continually remind each other that they, together, are the most important part of their marriage.

And if you have somebody that you can trust for two or three days with your children, a mini-vacation will do wonders for the marriage. On such a vacation, the two of you can be there only for each other, without chasing the children around. Some people will say that such a vacation may be too costly. I would like to tell you, however, that it will be more costly if you don't take time to do this.

Grace stayed at home while raising our three beautiful children. I was at work, sometimes running between two jobs. She got up with the kids, had breakfast with them, and played and entertained them all day when they were not in school. But the moment I put my foot in the door after work, she made sure to attend to my needs, without neglecting the children. She always made sure that dinner was ready and that I had a change of clothes if I had another job or task to attend to. And I always would try to help Grace with whatever she needed from me.

The best thing you can do for your children is not giving them toys or trying to make sure they have the best and the latest material things. The best thing you can do is show them you love your spouse and your spouse loves you. You should never be afraid to show your children how much affection there is between you and your spouse.

I remember when I was a kid, especially after lunch on the weekends, my mother would sit on my father's lap, and they would talk and giggle. For me, seeing them have such a good time together was one of my greatest times. Their display of loving intimacy gave me a great feeling of security. It showed me they had it together and would be there, together, for me.

There are many ways we can demonstrate to our spouse that he or she is our number-one priority. The way we treat and respect each other all day long is a major indicator. Do we keep in touch so that the other person knows where we are and what we are doing? If there is a change of plans, do we call? Do we, as men, open doors for our wives? Do we tell our spouse, every chance we get, how important he or she is to us? Even if a spouse knows he or she is important to the other, it still needs to be heard.

We must always remember that we, as individuals and as a couple, are a work in progress, and we must always be learning. If you haven't done some of these things, it is never too late to start.

Have you ever been served a meal you know is already delicious, but just because someone suggests you add salt and pepper to your food, you do? And you find it makes your food even more delicious. This is the kind of thing I am talking about. Even if your marriage is already good, adding the ingredients suggested previously will make your marriage even better. Even if you feel awkward at the beginning, do it anyway. It will soon become a comfortable habit.

I also believe it is important that you model these considerate behaviors for other couples. Maybe they will get the hint. There is nothing more beautiful to see than a couple who has it together and are not afraid to show it. My wife and I were in a wedding party recently, and three people approached us to say they could see the love all around us. It is certainly not a bad thing to be able to write about such comments after thirty-one years of marriage.

As your love grows over time, you are going to reach a level in your marriage that is incredible: the point when two people join together as truly one. You and your spouse no longer feel like different persons. You are almost always on the same wavelength. And whenever you are not together for some reason, you miss your spouse no matter what you are doing. The moment is not complete unless you are together, and when you are together, you do not need any outside events to be happy. Whatever you are doing together will make you happy. Such a feeling is awesome! I cannot tell you when this will take place in your marriage, but it will happen when you keep your spouse as your number-one priority during the good—and not so good—times.

March 6, 1979. With my family at the Uruguayan Airport the day that me and Grace's brother Angelo, came to the United States.

CHAPTER 7

Focus on the Good

Unless you have some health issues, have lost a job, or have lost a family member, most of what is happening in your life right now is good. You are healthy (or relatively healthy compared to other people), have your spouse, you may have kids, you have a place you call home, you have a job, food to eat, and at least one friend. You live in freedom in a great country.

But some of what is happening to you is not that good. You may have a health issue, you may not like your job, your kids might not be acting in accordance with your expectations, your house may need some repairs, or a person you thought was your friend stabs you in the back. Ouch!

In your marriage, most of what is happening between you and your spouse is great. You love each other, you enjoy each other, you are together, you have a family or are starting one, and you are not alone. But the rest of what goes on between the two of you could stand some improvement. This is usually the point at which you and your spouse have different ways of doing things. I like to put the toilet paper so it unrolls coming from the bottom, and my wife likes it coming from the top. I don't like the way she turns the steering wheel of the car before it starts moving; it is harder on the front wheels. She doesn't like the way I drive on curves. But we both realize that despite these minor differences, we are both okay. We are a work in progress.

The key concept is that what you focus on in life is what you will get more of. If you focus on the good in your marriage and life, you will attract more good things to you and your spouse. If we focus only on that not so good, you attract more of the same, and that will assume a giant role in our perceptions of daily life. If we focus only on what is not so good, the glass of our marriage will eventually overflow with things that will make us say, "That is enough. I am out of here." After a life in which we allowed ourselves to believe the grass is always greener on the other side, we will often discover too late the more attractive grass is artificial turf. It is plastic and dead.

It is not always easy to focus on the good stuff in our lives. The mind is always playing tricks on us to see how we will react. For instance, when you have something important that you know you have to do, it seems that you are going to get all kinds of distractions trying to deviate you from doing it. Every time that I thought that I had to write this book,

I found myself fighting with my mind distractions so that I could do it. Like: I have to cut the grass, fix the kitchen sink, change the oil in the car, etc. The challenge is to control our thoughts and bring them into alignment with our goals. Not only is it important to think right, we need to verbalize out loud to ourselves what we want to focus on and achieve. Have you ever ordered a to-go meal from a restaurant and when someone returned with your order, it wasn't what you wanted? You were upset and told the person who picked it up, "This is not what I ordered." The person who picked up your food showed you the paper you wrote your order on, and you realize you wanted one thing but wrote down another, and that's what you got. In life, it is important we write down exactly what we want and read it to ourselves every day until we get it. In other words, we have been programmed from the time we were in our crib to think in a negative way and to focus on the wrong things. We grow up hearing the word "no" far more often than the word "yes." We tend to pinpoint the negative aspects of other people rather than what is good about them. When we meet a stranger, our tendency is to look for something negative about the person so that we categorize them according to our negative beliefs.

Likewise, when we are married and have an argument or a disagreement with our spouse, our tendency is to say, "Aha, I knew it all along!" This is when we have to stop ourselves from thinking negatively. And while it might be difficult, this is the point where we have to allow ourselves to remember all the good things about our spouse. Perhaps making a list of five things you love about your spouse and taking a look at it will help you remember why you're together. Over time, how we react to the other person at critical points of disagreement will make or break our marriage. Are you filling the glass of your mind with a positive or negative view of your spouse? What you decide to fill your glass with will become the most powerful aspect of your relationship. The good news is you can decide every day to fill your glass with the positive. A man usually thinks from a long-term perspective, looking five to twenty years ahead. In general, a woman thinks more about now and the year ahead. Of course, sometimes it could be the other way around.

It is important to think long term and to visualize what you want to be doing twenty years from now. Regarding your marriage, imagine what you want your relationship to look like and what you would like to be doing together. I can easily imagine Grace and me, walking on a beautiful beach and holding hands. I can foresee myself with gray hair, a nice tan, and a smile on my face as I think about how I have become financially secure and how the kids are doing great in their adult lives. In short, I am enjoying life to the fullest.

When you can see a positive future for yourself and your spouse, it is much easier to deal with the difficult situations that may arise in your life right now. Imagine all the things you like to do together in the future, whether it be a vacation or a lifestyle. It is always up to us to choose the things we think about. When you and your spouse are upset with each other, try to work it out as soon as possible. It will be very helpful to have some ground rules.

For Example

- We'll refrain from name calling.
- Before we start talking, let's calm down.
- Perhaps one of us could take a walk for fifteen minutes.
- Let's start our talk with a prayer, asking God for guidance, and wait to discuss our problem until after we put the children to bed.

Why let a disagreement take away from your joy of life? Why not try to talk it out and move on? Recognizing your love for each other will do wonders in working toward a solution. Do not go to sleep upset with each other. Think about how you would feel if one of you did not wake up the next morning. Is that how you would want your relationship to end? Always say "I love you" before you go to sleep and when you wake up.

I am not saying you will not have problems with each other. There will be days when you and your spouse will look at each other and wonder what is going on. During such times, give each other space to get back to the way you would like to be. In difficult times, it is very important to return to your imagination and think about how you would like things to be in the future. It's very important that you both talk about what you would like your future together to be to make sure you are on the same track.

Just as a runner will close his or her eyes before a competitive event and imagine crossing the finish line first and being awarded the first place trophy, you must be able to form a mental picture of what you would like you and your spouse to be doing five, ten, or twenty years in the future. Doing so will help you overcome the difficulties of the present moment and give you guidance as to what you can do now to make things better.

Your mind acts just like a GPS; if you do not give it a destination, it doesn't matter whether you are going sideways, forward, or backward. The GPS will not direct you anywhere, because it has not been given a destination. You can waste a lot of precious time in such a directionless way. But the moment you give your GPS a specific destination, it will start working for you, telling you the best way to go in order to get where you want to go.

Without a goal—without a specific destination—your mind will work just like a GPS. Without a goal in mind, it does not really matter which way you are going with your life. But the moment you give your mind a destination, it will start working for you by helping you move in the direction of where you would like to be in five, ten, or twenty years. This is why setting goals is so important. People who set goals are always further ahead than everyone else. It just makes good sense to set goals.

I strongly suggest you stop reading after this chapter, and write down five goals that will help you improve your marriage.

Example

- I will start reading twenty minutes a day in a book about relationships.
- When I talk to my spouse, I will put everything else out of my mind and give my spouse my undivided attention.
- I will write down and think about all the things I love about my spouse.
- I will treat my spouse the way I did before we got married.
- I will find the time to tell my spouse how much I love him or her at least three times a day.

1980 with my parents and my great uncle Agripino.

CHAPTER
8

Intimacy

In the Scriptures (1 Corinthians 7:4) it is said that when a couple marries, his body is no longer his, but hers, and her body is no longer hers, but his. If you married for love and are treating each other with respect, I don't understand why this should be a problem. I have often heard it said that a woman becomes paralyzed from the waist down as soon as she gets married. But some intimacy problems occur because the husband doesn't know how to treat his wife so that he will get a good response.

We need to talk to each other about our sexual preferences and try to accommodate each other's needs as much as possible. We should never insist on doing anything that will satisfy only one partner. What you do needs to be fun for the both of you. Always talk about your likes and dislikes, and keep trying to improve your intimate relationship. I hear a lot of guys complain about their wives and who do not take care of them, especially in the area of intimacy. What is important is how you treat your wife all day long and not just the half hour before you are ready to go to bed with intentions. Here is one of the biggest differences between a man and his wife. I once heard a pastor talking about intimacy, and he said, "For a man, all it takes is to see his wife undress, and he is ready; for a woman, it is what a man has done all day that will turn her on or off."

At times suitable to intimacy, a wife will remember if you did not say good morning or give her a kiss before going off to work. She will remember if you talked to your neighbor instead of helping her unload a car full of groceries. She will remember if you got into the car first when it was raining, while she waited for you to unlock the door from the inside to allow her to get in. And she will certainly remember if she was cooking, washing clothes, ironing, cleaning house, and taking care of the children during the day, while you sat in your chair and watched TV all day and did not offer to help her.

In such circumstances, my friend, you are going to pay for it. Even if she does get intimate with you, she will not give you her best, and you will think you will feel alone even though you are together.

Don't make sexual intimacy a monotonous job. This is the ultimate moment in a couple's relationship, and it should be enjoyable. Don't deprive each other sexually unless one is sick. If one of you has the desire for intimacy, it should be enough to be together as an act of love. Is not love about taking care of each other? It is not about awarding points to see if sexual intimacy has been earned.

There is nothing more special in a marriage that is based on love than to give to each other completely. It is very important to go to bed with each other at the same time at night. If a spouse waits until the other is sound asleep to come to bed, the chances of intimacy will go way down. There are many ways for intimacy to happen between human beings, but there is only one way that is the right way. The way that will give you both total enjoyment is to be intimate within a marital relationship, when both are madly in love and committed to enjoying each other. When this happens, you will feel right, and you will feel great.

Men are conquerors by nature—hunters, if you will. So some men think in order to be a real man, they need to have more than one mate, even when in the state of matrimony. But the truth is that a real man is one who is married to the one person he loves, and he is dedicated to making his marriage work.

When you buy a house or car, you gather all of the facts about it, and when you buy it, you feel good about it and stop looking. Once you have married the person you know is going to make you happy for the rest of your life, you should stop looking. You already have what you were looking for. If you are in a marriage that is going really bad, you must first try to do everything within your power to work it out: talk to each other, read books, attend seminars or counseling sessions. Before considering a way out, it is important both of you do the things necessary to keep the marriage together.

February 1980, the day I won the lottery. Our Wedding in Montevideo, Uruguay. I was twenty and she was nineteen. We got married in a Catholic Church.

CHAPTER
9

Always Keep Improving You

One key to improving your marriage is to improve yourself. In my seminars on living a balanced life, I explain that we, as human beings, operate on three levels: physical, mental, and spiritual. Unless we are continually working on these three areas, it is going to be difficult to triumph when things get tough. When married life is not going the way you dream of, you will be better able to deal with it if you are physically, mentally, and spiritually in shape.

When engineers design a plane, they closely calculate the weight, wing length, engine thrust, and the speed necessary for liftoff. All of this is necessary for the plane to take off and stay aloft. If the plane needs to take off at three hundred miles per hour but doesn't achieve that speed on the runaway, the results will be unsatisfactory if not catastrophic. The same goes for us. If we do not attend to our physical, mental, and spiritual aspects, we won't be able to take off.

The Physical Part of Life

We all know many people ignore the physical aspect of life. Not only is achieving and maintaining good health important, keeping your physical appearance will also help you feel good about yourself. Around December, many people start their list of resolutions by stating, "I am going to start exercising in January." So they buy some sophisticated equipment, like a treadmill, bike, or rowing machine. Do you know the best time to purchase a piece of used exercise equipment that is virtually new? It is in April, when people with good intentions put ads in the paper to sell their equipment. In fact, some of it is still in the original boxes.

In theory, the idea of exercising sounds good, and we know what to do, but it is very hard to bring ourselves to do it. Well, I will tell you why. At the point when Eve gave the apple to Adam, sin entered the human body, and our body developed a desire to do what is bad for us. The body, on its own, is lazy; it wants to do nothing, sleep all day, eat all day, smoke, and drink.

Here is the key. Either you master your body or your body will master you. While the body will not like it, we need to exercise a minimum of three times per week for thirty minutes per session. If you have never exercised or it has been a long time since you've done so, make sure you check with your doctor to see what you can safely do before beginning.

Find some kind of exercise that you like. Do something that will make you break a sweat, like running, biking, rowing, basketball, soccer, swimming, or some other aerobic exercise.

One time, I was flipping channels and happened to see Richard Simmons. What got my attention was that he was helping people in wheelchairs exercise. He told them, "Whatever you can do to move, do it, because it will bring some benefit to you."

When you are tired all of the time, it is probably because your energy level is low. When you buy an electronic gadget with rechargeable batteries, you are instructed to wear the batteries all the way down, so they will recharge with maximum energy. Well, we are the same way. If you don't exercise and use a lot of energy, you will not fully recharge with new energy. This is why people who exercise a lot are generally so bubbly and ready to go.

When I took a Dale Carnegie course, the one thing that stuck with me the most is the idea that feeling follows action, and not the other way around. Most people wait to exercise until they feel like it, so it is most likely not going to happen. It is not until you are exercising on a regular basis that your body will automatically want to exercise. When you take action, your feelings will catch up to it.

Do you remember when you were younger and you had to go to practice when you may not have felt like going? But you went anyway. I'll bet that after fifteen minutes of practice, you were happy you were there. That is because you took action, and your feelings caught up with it. Successful people are very aware of this principle. They don't listen to their feelings; they just take action.

But it is important for you to be patient with yourself. If you haven't exercised in a long time, don't expect to be back in shape in one or two months. It may take three or four months—or even longer—of consistent exercise before you begin to feel and look better.

Looking for the fountain of youth? People who exercise consistently look younger than their actual age. And remember that when you feel good about yourself, you will most likely attract good things into your life. You have to make appointments with yourself to exercise, and make sure you exercise at the same time and on the same days. Exercise must become a priority. I exercise Tuesdays, Thursdays, and Saturdays at the same time. If someone wants to see you when you have an appointment with yourself to exercise, you should tell them you are busy and schedule another time to see them. The best way to have consistency is to create a pattern and stick to it.

Whenever I hear of a television program that is positive, I try to watch it. Not too long ago, I watched a program about people throughout the world who lived to be over one hundred years of age. The common denominator is that they all did some type of exercise, whether it was with machines or walking outside. What a surprise! But it is never too late to get started. It doesn't matter how old you are. You could be eighty years old today and have another twenty-five years to live. Or you could be sixteen years old and have only two more years to live. Unless you know when you are going to die, age does not matter.

Studies have also determined that for the body, it is best to go to bed early and to get up early. Get good rest; seven to eight hours of sleep are best.[4] I also like to take multivitamins.

If you have a brand-new Cadillac, would you put kerosene in the gas tank instead of gasoline? If you did, the engine would probably not run and may be broken down forever. Well, if you wouldn't try to run a car on an inappropriate fuel, why would you smoke or put drugs in your body? Here is the question: How important are you to you? If you are important to yourself, wouldn't you take care of yourself?

If you smoke, write down on a piece of paper why smoking is good for you. Unless you sell cigarettes, I don't know why you would do that to yourself. We all know that cigarettes are bad for us. In 1 Corinthians 3:16-17, we were told to take care of your temple. Every time I visit a temple, no

---

[4] "I know what to do, so why don't I do it?" The New Science of Self Discipline. By Nick Hall, PH. D.

matter where in the world, I am impressed by the magnificent size and decoration that people took the time to put together when creating a lasting presence. How are we taking care of our own temple?

I believe you should be more aware of your percentage of body fat than your actual weight. This is called the body mass index (BMI). When you buy a scale that reads both your weight and your body fat percentage, it comes with a manual that will tell you, based on your age and height, what your BMI should be according to medical experts. This is, I think, a more accurate way of gauging your physical condition. You can have two guys who are both 6'3" and weigh 280 pounds, but one is a football player with only 18 percent body fat, and the other is a sedentary person with a fat percentage of 43 percent. Only one of these persons would be considered out of shape despite the fact they weigh the same.

You should always check with your doctor before trying to lose weight. But unless you have a physical condition, losing weight shouldn't be so complicated. So why is it so difficult to know how to lose weight? You take in calories by eating and drinking; you expend calories by moving. If you take in more calories than you are burn, guess what? You gain weight in fat. We are all different, and so are our bodies. In general, the answer to weight loss is to exercise more and eat less if you want to reduce your fat content. Weight loss pills are effective only when accompanied by exercise; and they should only be used under medical supervision. You need to be able to visualize how you want to look.

How important are you to you? You only have one life to live, and the clock is always ticking. Start today! The benefits of being in shape are immeasurable: you look great, you feel great, and you feel like doing more. Everybody is unique, and with the right amount of effort, you can bring out the best in yourself.

Many years ago, the Roman government asked a famous sculptor to create something unique that would define Rome as a special city. The Romans gave him a giant square of marble that was stored in a great warehouse. When they brought him to look at it, the sculptor did not like it, because it had a big crack running through it. When he refused to work with the flawed marble, the Roman officials were devastated and didn't know what to do. The government officials thought only of the embarrassment that would come to the city due to the sculptor's rejection. One of the officials remembered there was another sculptor, who was not as famous, and they decided to ask him what he could do with the giant marble. The new sculptor looked at the marble closely and thought about it deeply before he finally said, "Yes, I will do something with it."

He grabbed a hammer and a chisel and started working on it. Months went by before he announced he was done and called the Roman authorities to come and look at it. When they came to the warehouse, the officials saw a beautiful statue of a naked man. Today, this statue of King David is one of the most famous ones in the world. The artist, Michelangelo, became well known to all.

I believe in each of us there is a statue of a king or a queen who is the real you. But just like Michelangelo, we need to work with the materials, however flawed, with which we have been provided. By exercising, reading books, and listening to self-help materials, we are like Michelangelo, using his hammer and chisel to take away those parts that are unneeded or flawed in order to reveal the greatness within each of us.

I believe that our great God did not go through so much trouble to give us a brain and a body for us to live a mediocre life. What you are is a gift from God, and whatever you make out of yourselves is your gift to God. So what are you going to do with what you have? Some of us have bigger flaws than others, but so what? It is time to make the lemonade out of whatever lemons you have been given and to drink it too. We are all given a hand of cards, some better than others, but that is what we have. What are you going to do to make a positive change in your life? It could be in your physical, mental, or spiritual aspect of your life. Whatever you do affects everything else in your life. Any improvement is going to make a positive impact on your total being. Start with a simple task, such as walking around the block or eating an apple a day, and this will propel you to do more for yourself in all other areas.

Always try to look your best.

- Work on yourself; dress up for every occasion. Men should put on a suit and tie once in a while and have a nice blazer and khakis for less-formal occasions. Make sure your hair is cut nicely.
- Keep your spouse excited about being married to you. This advice goes for men and women alike. Keep in shape and exercise regularly. There is no excuse for not doing so.
- Always look your best for each other. You become the best you can for her, and she becomes the best she can for you.
- Always try to improve your appearance, because this will keep alive the excitement and desire for each other.

The Mental Part of Life

The mental part of life encompasses our thoughts, which influence our attitude and determine how we live our lives. In my talks I often ask the audience, "How many of you believe your mind plays a very important part in your life?" Without hesitation, everybody raises their hand. Then I ask a second question: "How many of you, in the last six months, have read a book, gone to a seminar, or watched a DVD about how to improve your mind?" Well, at that point, only about 3 to 5 percent of the hands are raised. Then I ask the question again to emphasize the point that this could be an indicator of how well the lives of audience members are going.

You see, life never stops; the clock is always ticking. We are either getting ahead, or we are falling behind. There is no middle point here. You tell me your mind plays a very important part in your life, yet you haven't taken the time to learn how to use it. Isn't that strange?

After being in this country a couple of years, I thought people did not like me because I was a foreigner. I didn't speak the language, Cleveland was cold, and I even blamed the government for my situation. Someone saw me pointing the finger of blame and told me, "Look at your fingers. You are pointing out with one finger, but three fingers are pointing back. Your own hand is saying your problems are your fault by a ratio of three to one." Then this person had the audacity to tell me that if I took care of my own attitude, things would get better for me. He told me that my attitude would determine my altitude and that 85 percent of whatever happens in my life depends on my attitude. This was when I was introduced to self-help materials.

As it turned out, when my attitude improved, my circumstances also improved. It was well worth the effort I had to make to improve my attitude and my conditions. Back then, reading was very difficult for me. With a second-grade reading level in English, how was I going to read books that were designed to help me? But with the encouragement of a great group of people I met through a multilevel company, I pushed myself and started to read. I also listened to tapes and went to seminars on self-improvement.

I began to develop a sense of self-confidence again, and all of a sudden, I thought that maybe I could do something really great in this country. Then in one of many self-improvement seminars, I had a brilliant idea. What if one day I could become a speaker and try to help other people as these presenters were helping me? I became addicted to self-improvement. I am still addicted, and I love it.

For the past twenty-seven years, I have been reading and listening to tapes, DVDs, and radio and TV programs related to self-improvement. I took a Dale Carnegie course and was selected to be a teaching assistant. Eventually, I was asked by the Dale Carnegie organization to become a teacher, but this required a college education, which I did not have.

How much is our mind worth? One million? Ten million? Ten billion? It is priceless. We can do so many things with our mind, yet we take it for granted. We admire a camera with zoom and wide lenses. Yet our eyes are capable of zooming in on little objects or viewing things like a landscape from a wide perspective without even thinking about it.

Our mind regulates our temperature, controls our breathing, and instructs our hearts to maintain a regular heart rate. If we cut ourselves, our mind sends a message to our body to start healing itself immediately. Because of our mind, we hear, taste, and smell.

But your mind is only worth what you think it is. "As a man thinks he is in his heart, so is he." Proverbs 23:7 This is a revelation given to man by God. How much are you worth? Most people will look at their checking account and say, "I have $375; I guess that is what I am worth." You will become worth only what you think you are worth. If you think you are worth only what is in your checking account, that is all you will be worth.

What if I told you there is something that has never been made before, it's one of a kind, and will never be made again? How could we put a price on something that is so unique? If sold, it probably would be at a price in the billions. What if I told you that this precious thing is you?

You are unique; the only you that will ever be made. You are a special individual, an edition of one. You cannot compare yourself to anybody, because we are all different. The mind you have inside you is the only one that has ever existed. You are great; God created you and said, "It is good." When you realize how special you truly are, you will believe you deserve a great life with a great marriage, and things will start to unfold for you in the direction you and your partner want to go together.

I believe the more you watch TV, the smaller your income will be; the more that you read, the more you will earn. Which one will you choose? The little choices will make the difference. We will make only a few really big choices in our lives—which career to pursue, who to marry, what house to purchase, and so on. However, you will be faced with hundreds of little choices every day that will really shape your life: whether to exercise, whether to read or watch TV, what to drink and eat, and so on.

A house occupied by a family with kids running around all day will experience a lot of wear and tear. But we all know a house that is left empty will deteriorate a lot faster, because, after all, a house is built to be used. Likewise, when you use a car all of the time, it will wear out. The tires, breaks, engine, and transmission will all get worn. But if that same car is left parked and unused, it will deteriorate a lot faster. A car is meant to be driven, not parked.

When we read, go to seminars, take classes, and work on developing our minds, our brains get used a lot, and we may feel tired. But like a house or car, our brains, if not used regularly, will deteriorate faster than if used regularly. We have been given an incredible brain to use, and we have to use it to our advantage.

We cannot worry about what people think, because other people are worried about themselves and not thinking about you. The only brain you can improve is your own. How important are you to you? Here is the answer to many of the questions you may have about your life. If you are important to you, you will take care of yourself in every dimension of your life.

- Pray: ask God to help you throughout the day.
    - Do so as soon as you can in the morning.
    - Pray every time you get in your car or catch a bus.

- Count your blessings every day.
    - Write down at least ten things you are grateful for, and read them every morning to start your day.

- Stay away from negative media, friends, and coworkers.
    - Read a chapter of a self-help book every day or listen to a CD in your car to stimulate your positive thinking.

- When a negative thought comes into your mind, don't entertain it; immediately replace it with a positive thought.

- Focus on the positive in every situation 'til it becomes your habit.
- Find a seminar to attend where being positive is the main theme.

If you think all of this costs money, it will cost you more money in the long run if you don't do them. Believe me. You are directly investing in yourself, and that is the best investment anybody can make.

The Spiritual Part of Life

God is the glue that will keep marriage together. I'll begin with a story of how God works in our lives.

There was a man who built his own plane. It had a single engine and two seats. One afternoon he decided to take it out for a flight over the ocean. After all, it was a beautiful summer day, and the sky was a clear blue. He was enjoying a great flight, when he encountered some turbulence. His engine, for no reason he could think of, suddenly lost all power. To the right was a small island, and the pilot tried to steer the plane toward it. All he could think of was, *God, don't let me die.* Luckily, with just the right wind conditions, he was able to land the plane in shallow waters close to the shore of the island. He had just enough time to get off the plane and swim to the tiny beach. Looking back, he saw his plane sink into the dark waters of the ocean.

Night came on quickly, but the stranded pilot was sure the Coast Guard would be looking for him. Over the coming days, he waited and waited, but nobody showed up to save him. He began to get desperate and constantly thought about his loved ones. He was able to eat fruits and vegetables, and also learned how to fish. Three months passed, and he realized nobody was coming for him. One day, out of desperation, he got on his knees and asked God to help him to get him off that little island before he died there. To his surprise, the pilot heard a voice from the sky say to him, "See that round rock at the end of the beach; I want you to roll it to the beach on the other side of the island." The pilot was speechless, but he was not going to question these instructions. So he got behind the round rock and started to push it. But it was so heavy that he could not make it move. The man tried repeatedly without success until he fell asleep right next to it.

When he woke in the morning, he immediately got behind the rock and tried to push it again. This time, he was able to move it slightly. By the end of the day, he had only been able to move it about one foot before he fell asleep. He did the same thing every day. For months he worked at moving the rock, but by the end of the fifth month, he had moved it only one hundred feet. He was ready to quit. He said, "This is ridiculous. What am I doing, pushing this rock anyway? What am I accomplishing?"

The voice came back to him and said, "Now look at your legs." He hadn't noticed, but his legs had grown big and strong. The voice then instructed, "Look at your arms and back. Now that you are strong and ready, I can show you how to construct a canoe, so you can row back to your homeland."

I believe this story presents a very common situation. We get on our knees and ask God to move us to a better house, job, or relationship. But in order for us to get to a better place, God needs to work on us to get us ready for the improvement we have asked him for. When things get tough, we start complaining and may even ask to go back to where we were when we first called out to God for help. God often says, "Okay, do whatever you want." This is when we really get into trouble. Can you see yourself in this story? It is time to believe God works for us, not against us.

I am an amateur when it comes to the spiritual dimension of life, but I have done a lot of research in this area and have tried to learn as much as possible. All I can share with you, the reader, is what I have learned and how I try to experience a spiritual life. I deliberately said "try," because I believe most people—including me—fall short when it comes to spirituality.

Not only do I believe there is a God, I also believe God is powerful, loving, wise, caring, immense, perfect, and capable of doing anything at any time. "With God, all things are possible" (Matthew 19:26). If you don't have God in your life, you won't have love and wisdom, because these things come only from God.

I am a Christian, which means I believe that Jesus is the Son of God, who gave his life for us to pay our debts so that we can be free of sin and live a wonderful life. It is hard to believe God created us with the will to pursue perfection. If you study how our body works in an automatic mode to care for itself, I think you will be convinced that only God could pull this off.

I don't think we were created by God with all the tools we have at our disposal in order to live a life of misery, quiet desperation, depression, poverty, and suffering. We were not created to be stuck in place, especially when it is a bad place. We were created to live a life of happiness, enjoyment, success, and fulfillment. Why do most people not realize these positive aspects of life?

I think when God created us, he didn't just put us on the planet and say, "Well, good luck. I have given you dominion over the planet—over plants and animals—and good luck in figuring out how to use these things." I believe God created us with the ability to take care of all the problems we encounter in exercising freedom and making good choices. At the same time, we don't always make the best choices in exercising our freedom and freewill.

If you have problems with your car, you take it to a mechanic. If you have problems with your computer, you find a good IT person. If you have problems with your teeth, you go to a dentist. If you have problems with your heart, you go to a doctor. When it comes to our lives, instead of going to the expert, we talk to our family, friends, or coworkers. In most cases, they do not know the answer. Sometimes they have more problems than you do, and sometimes they are kind of glad your problems are worse than theirs. It makes them feel not so bad about their own problems.

Working in the electrical trade, I used to think I could fix anything that came with wires without any problems. Several years ago, when we bought our first VCR, I stood in front of our TV, with the remote in my hands. The VCR was not working. My wife asked me, "Why don't you get the manual?" Being an electrician, I thought I did not need the manual and could figure it out on my own. Fifteen minutes went by, and I still could not figure it out. My wife again asked me, "Why don't you read the manual?" Finally, when my wife went outside, I got the manual, read it, and had the VCR running properly in fewer than five minutes. I had wasted twenty minutes trying to do it, as Frank Sinatra sang, "my way."

Again, I want to emphasize that God did not just put us on this planet and say, "Good luck. I will be watching you." God gave us all the instructions we need to accomplish whatever we want in this life and the ability to find a solution to any problem we may encounter.

I have a hard time understanding how most people can find the time to read about their car, computer, and smart phone, but they never seem to find the time to read the instruction manual for their own lives. And then they wonder why they are living unsatisfied lives, going nowhere, and are burned out by the age of forty-five.

We possess a manual that tells us if we take certain actions, we will get certain results. There is not a single situation in the world that is not in the manual. All the answers are there. For me, my manual is the Holy Bible, where God not only gives me all of the directions I will ever need but also provides examples of people who were in the process of learning what to do and what not to do. Why would anyone waste their precious life without reading the manual they have been given by God in order to make the most out of their lives?

In reading the Bible, I start on page 1 of the Old Testament and read it all the way through, a few pages a day. I don't read super-fast; I try to digest what I read. English is my second language. What is your excuse? I am not an expert. I am a student who is trying to get the most out of my life.

The way people are will never change. What will change are the material things around us, especially our technology.

But we human beings are always the same, and God knows that. This is why the manual does not change. It is and will always be up to date.

Prayer is our way of communication with God. It is a wireless system that has been around for thousands of years. This is what I do; I pray as a Catholic Christian. I try to participate in mass once a week. I became a Eucharistic minister about fifteen years ago. I don't just sit there at mass; I like to participate. This allows me to be more connected and grow deeper within my faith. I encourage you to find ways to do the same with your religion. If you do not have a religion, I recommend visiting and learning about different denominations to see where you feel at home. You can start by asking God to help you find the right place for you.

Mass is also a way of giving testimony of our faith to the Christian community. I love the mass and the people in my congregation. I always get something out of it. When Jesus gave the bread and wine to his followers, he said, "Do this in remembrance of me." I take this very seriously.

I read the Bible once a day; I pray from the time that I wake up. Before I leave my house in the morning, I make sure I get on my knees and pray. My prayers are layered like a sandwich: express gratitude, ask for help, and be grateful. For example, I follow what Jesus taught us by starting with the prayer, "Our Father." Then I thank God for all the things He has given me, such as my family, my health, my job, my house, and anything I think of that is good for me. Next I ask God for the wisdom, love, discipline, sense of humor, and anything else I think I need at the moment. Finally, I thank God for all he has given me and for what he is going to give me.

I am grateful for what I already have: my health, my family, and my life in general. I ask for wisdom and the discipline to accomplish whatever I have to do. I mention the names of all of the people I pray for. I pray for the president of the United States and leaders throughout the world so that they have the wisdom to do what is right for everyone. I pray for any particular situation I am dealing with.

Every time I have to speak in front of groups, I pray I can be a window for God to pass his wisdom to the people and that they will receive it. I also try to be a mirror that reflects God's love. This is why I never take credit for anything I say; the credit goes to God. I am merely the messenger who has been given the opportunity to do what I love so much.

I pray every time I start driving, whether I am alone or with others. Every time I take a long trip, I pray. I close each of my prayers with an expression of gratitude for all God has given me and for all he will give me in the future. The reason I am describing this now is not to demonstrate how holy I am or anything like that. I am just describing what I do in terms of prayer, because I know there are a lot of people who do not know where to begin in living their lives in a spiritual way. Perhaps this will give those people an idea. There are no set rules for our conversation with God; he created you, he knows you, and like any father, he wants what is best for you.

I believe that, like a parent, God wants the very best for you. He will give you what you need if you listen to him and if you meet him halfway in whatever you do. God says, "When you move, I move." If you ask but do not do your part, God won't do his part. When you pray, believe it and go for it, and he will give you whatever is good in life. We are always striving to put God first in our lives. If we do that, we can't go wrong in any area of our lives.

I believe our lives are meant to be lived and enjoyed. And we should do all that we can in making this work. Some people try to live as little as possible. If this is what we do with our lives, I believe we will, at some point, look back on our lives and wish we had done more.

August of 1989, with our precious kids. From left to right.
Daniela, Jacqueline and Marcos.

CHAPTER 10

Keep Improving Your Marriage

We don't know everything or even know most things. Once we accept that we always need to find ways to improve ourselves physically, mentally, and spiritually, we are on the right path. In the fine libraries we have in this country, there is a self-help section, my favorite part of a library. In the books, CDs, and DVDs we find in this section, we can find the benefit of the wisdom of people who have spent many years researching ways people can improve their lives. Their experience and knowledge are readily available for you without spending years of doing the research yourself.

Whenever Grace and I find a good book on relationships, we read it. We want to make sure we are becoming the best we can for each other. The best thing you can do for your spouse is to become the best person you can. Of course, you cannot give what you don't have, but if you are willing to learn and admit you don't know everything, the two of you can become better people for each other for all time.

If you think you cannot afford a good seminar on marriage and relationships, you cannot afford not to go to one of them. There are also retreats for married couples. Marriage should be so much fun; if your marriage is not fun, you need to work at it.

Place God first, family second, and everything else after that. This should be our aim in life. Sometimes we deviate from the right path, but like an airplane, we should try to stay on course. If we do so, we will arrive at the end of our lives happy and content. May God bless you!

February 2005, we renewed our vows with the captain of the Carnival cruise, celebrating our twenty-fifth anniversary in the Caribbean.

Suggested Readings

Adler, Mortimer Jerome, and Charles Van Doren. How to read a book. New York: Simon and Schuster, 1972.

Byrne, Rhonda. The secret. New York: Atria Books;, 2006.

Carnegie, Dale. How to win friends & influence people. New York: Pocket Books, 1981.

Chapman, Gary D. The five love languages: how to express heartfelt commitment to your mate. Chicago: Northfield Pub., 1995.

Helmstetter, Shad. What to say when you talk to your self. Wellingborough: Thorsons, 1991.

Hill, Napoleon. Think and grow rich / By Napoleon Hill. Greenwich, Conn.: Fawcett Publications, 1960.

Holy Bible: the new King James version, containing the Old and New Testaments. Nashville: T. Nelson, 1982.

Johnson, Spencer. Who moved my cheese?: an a-mazing way to deal with change in your work and in your life. New York: Putnam, 1998.

Mandino, Og. The greatest secret in the world; featuring your own success recorder diary with the ten great scrolls for success from The greatest salesman in the world. New York: F. Fell, 1972.

Nightingale, Earl. Earl Nightingale's greatest discovery: "the strangest secret—revisited.". New York: Dodd, Mead, 1987.

Osteen, Joel. Every day a Friday: how to be happier 7 days a week. New York, NY: FaithWords, 2011.

Peale, Norman Vincent. Enthusiasm makes the difference. Englewood Cliffs, N.J.: Prentice-Hall, 1967.

Rohn, Jim, E. James Rohn, and Chris Widener. Twelve pillars: a novel. Irving, TX: Jim Rohn International and Chris Widener International, 2005.

Schwartz, David Joseph. The magic of thinking big. New York: Simon & Schuster, 1965.

Ziglar, Zig. Over the top moving from survival to stability, from stability to success, from success to significance. Nashville, Tenn.: Thomas Nelson, 1997.